Journal of an ADHD Kid

Journal
of an
ADHD Kid

THE GOOD, THE BAD, AND THE USEFUL

Tobias Stumpf
with Dawn Schaefer Stumpf

2014 ■ WOODBINE HOUSE

Published in the United States of American by Woodbine House, Inc.,

6510 Bells Mill Road, Bethesda, MD 20817. 800-843-7323.

www.woodbinehouse.com.

Illustrations by Gary Mohrman

Library of Congress Cataloging-in-Publication Data

Stumpf, Tobias.

Journal of an ADHD kid : the good, the bad, and the useful / Tobias Stumpf ; with Dawn Schaefer Stumpf. -- Revised edition.

pages cm

Includes bibliographical references and index.

Audience: 12-13

ISBN 978-1-60613-250-0 (pbk. : alk. paper) 1. Stumpf, Tobias--Diaries--Juvenile literature. 2. Attention-deficit hyperactivity disorder--Juvenile literature. 3. Attention-deficit-disordered children--Diaries--Juvenile literature. 4. Attention-deficit-disordered children--Family relationships--Juvenile literature. I. Stumpf, Dawn Schaefer. II. Title.

RJ506.H9S79 2014

618.92'8589--dc23

2014024699

Dedicated to all real kids like me with ADHD and their parents.

—Toby Stumpf

Dedicated to: my son, brave enough to share his thoughts, ideas, and journey; my family, Jim, Talia, and our parents, for being a supportive family filled with love; and the ADHD support group moms who gather to share, support, and shine on!

—Dawn Schaefer Stumpf

TABLE OF CONTENTS

INTRODUCTION:
A LETTER TO YOU!

Dear Real Kids (or anyone else reading this book),

    I'm Toby. (That's Toby with a **y** not an **i**. I'll get to that later!) I'm a real kid just like you. I have ADHD, inattentive type. I have also dealt with anxiety, tics, OCD... (These things are usually a "mixed bag!")

    One day I was reading **The Diary of a Wimpy Kid,** by Jeff Kinney. His book gave me this idea to write in a journal (I can't stand the word **diary**) about having ADHD. See, I never really liked talking about having ADHD. Neither did any of my friends. I thought that talking to a journal would be a great way to get over not wanting to talk about it. It worked. It was easier talking to a journal and it helped me better understand me, a real kid with ADHD.

After writing stuff in my journal, I started feeling better about having ADHD. I wasn't as worried about what others might think about me. Most of all, I began sharing some stuff with my friends, and I learned that there are A LOT OF US out there with ADHD (kids and adults).

The point of this book is to help kids just like me. I'd like you to know that there are tons of kids who have ADHD and it's OKAY to talk about it! I'd love to talk to you...but there are so many of you that it might be easier if you just read my journal. I bet that there are parts in here that'll make you say... "Hey, that's a lot like me!" Even though everyone with ADHD is different, a lot of our experiences might be the same. So, check it out. Find out how we're alike and how we're different. Then, you can use the journal pages after each section to "talk to me."

I hope you enjoy the book. There have been many times I almost threw it away. One time I even

tossed it into a fire and my mom had to dig it out.
Just shows, I'm not really sure that what I have to
say is worth much...but I do know that I am a real
kid with ADHD. I have a lot to say about having
ADHD, even though I don't like to talk about it.
Maybe you feel like that too?

A real kid like you,

Toby

TOBY WITH A Y:
NORMAL AND NOT

Dear Journal,

    Hi, my name's Toby. That's Toby with a **y**. My mom says it should be spelled with an **i**, but I use a **y**. As you can see, my mom and I don't always agree on things. For example, I have ADHD, and my mom says that having ADHD is pretty normal for lots of kids and can be a gift. I don't always think so! Sometimes I think I'm the only kid in the world with ADHD. I don't feel very normal.

    What is normal anyway? I like to skateboard. That's pretty normal for a kid my age. I ride my bike, go to school, play video games. (But not too many. My mom says they're not good for me.) I play football, basketball, and golf. I do my homework and practice my guitar. (My mom makes me.) See, pretty normal stuff!

Yet, ADHD makes me feel not so normal. You see, sometimes I get off track. I was just writing in this journal and then a big noise happened and I forgot what I was doing. Forgetting what I need to do happens to me all the time in school too! That's bad, especially when a teacher expects me to get something done.

Sometimes I forget to think before I do things, and that gets me into trouble. Like the time I wanted to spray paint a cardboard box silver to make it look like a robot. I thought it would be a good idea to paint it in the garage. I didn't want to let the stink out, so I closed all the garage doors. What I didn't think about is that not letting the stink out kept the stink in, and that's DANGEROUS! My mom kinda had a fit about me not thinking before I did that! My dad was kinda mad too 'cause spraying in the garage meant that our white car had some new silver paint splattered on it now. OOPS!

As an ADHD'r, I take medicine every day. It's annoying! This doesn't make me feel normal either. But my parents say I need it because it helps me think things through before I do them and helps me to not forget stuff. So, I take my meds and hope they'll help me this next year in school.

I'm in middle school. School's pretty cool. You get to see your friends, learn some interesting stuff. My school's pretty much a normal school, except for Millie, the ghost that lives on the third floor. My mom says Millie's not real. She went to the same school. That was long ago, so I don't think she knows much, and I don't agree with her!

Anyway, I'm Toby with a y, not an i. I'm a normal kid and I have ADHD.

Totally normal,

Toby

WHAT ARE SOME "NORMAL" THINGS ABOUT YOU?

ARE THERE TIMES YOU DON'T FEEL NORMAL?

WHEN?

WHY?

SO YOU THINK I HAVE ADHD?

Dear Journal,

I was pretty young when my teacher talked to my parents about some "concerns" she had about my learning and behaviors in school. I was about eight and in second grade.

My teacher said I could do second grade stuff just fine, but I was super slow to get done. She said I was a good and kind kid, but I was always getting in other kids' space and doing goofy things that got me into trouble.

One day the teacher wrote a note home to tell my parents that I had trouble walking to lunch. Who gets into trouble walking to lunch? I guess I do. The teacher said that I walked in circles and kept running into people. I guess I had trouble knowing where my personal space bubble was. She also said that it didn't look like I paid attention when she was talking to the class. It was hard for my parents to hear these things. If you ask them about it, my mom will say, "It was a very hard year."

Everyone's different. Some kids have lots of energy and move around like they have a motor that they can't slow down. These kids are hyper. Some kids are always the first ones to shout out answers in school. It's like their mouth is a volcano that's exploding. Then there are kids that have their heads up in outer space. They get called on in class and all they can say is "Huh?" I even know of kids who hide their faces behind their books hoping the teacher won't call on them. These kids worry they won't know the right answer. I've had worries like that too!

Anyway, everyone's different. That doesn't mean they have a disability or—like we sometimes call it in our house—a "differbility!" Like I said,

I sometimes had those worries and hid behind my book, and other times I was like the kid with his head in outer space. I had trouble getting jobs done, and I had a hard time paying attention. So the big people in my world wondered if something was wrong. They wondered if I had ADHD (Attention Deficit Hyperactivity Disorder).

So, you think I have ADHD? Well...it eventually took lots of different people to figure it out! My teacher had paperwork to do, like filling in checklists that told the doctor if I got my work done or had trouble paying attention in class. The school nurse came into my class and watched me work. My parents made lots of different doctor appointments...with the eye doctor, my regular doctor, doctors that help with diet, and special doctors like psychologists.

People can't just say, "You have ADHD." It takes time and a lot of different people working together to figure out what's going on in a brain like mine. I am thankful that my parents, teachers, and doctors took the time to figure it all out. It made me feel like I was important and that people wanted to help me be my best.

So, you think I have ADHD?

Toby

WHEN AND WHY DID PEOPLE START TO WONDER IF
YOU HAD ADHD?

DID YOU EVER FEEL LIKE SOMETHING WAS
"DIFFERENT" ABOUT YOU?

IF SO...WHY? WHAT THINGS DID YOU DO THAT MADE
YOU FEEL "DIFFERENT"?

IF YOU REMEMBER, HOW DID YOU FEEL ABOUT ALL
THE CONCERNS PEOPLE HAD ABOUT YOU?

Did you...

☐ Feel as mad as a stepped-on rattlesnake
   and want your teacher to slither away?

☐ Feel embarrassed or confused like you
   wanted to hide up in a tree like a sloth?

☐ Feel happy that you got to skip out of class
   for doctor appointments (and usually an ice
   cream treat after)?

☐ I felt...

TAKING THE TESTS

Dear Journal,

I was in second grade when I started making trips to see different doctors. First, it was my regular-everyday doctor. You know, the one you go to for sore throats and shots. After a visit with her, we made an appointment with a doctor who tries to see if what you eat is making you do the things you do. I had to try all kinds of different things...like not eating anything with wheat or red food dye. My parents hoped that would make things better, but it didn't, so then they made an appointment for me with a psychologist. A psychologist is a doctor who specializes in how our brains work and how we behave.

The psychologist I saw was pretty cool. She had funky puzzles on her table that I could play with while she talked or while my mom and dad talked. At first, I was a little worried about seeing this psychologist and taking tests. I thought the tests might be like school tests. Some were. I had to do some math and reading stuff, but it was never super hard stuff. It was all the stuff I already knew from school.

A bunch of the tests were actually really fun. Some tests were puzzles. One was even on a computer that was just like playing a video game! I really liked the part of the tests when the doctor got out blocks and I got to build stuff.

The tests were pretty painless and we didn't have to do them all in one day. My parents were really nice to me and would take me out for an ice cream treat or something fun afterwards.

The cool thing about the tests was...it didn't matter how I did. I wasn't going to fail anything like you might in school. Instead, the tests told the doctors (and me and my family) more about me. The tests told us things like how my brain works, how I learn best, and what I'm good at.

In school, it seems like there's always a test to take now and then. It's the same at the doctor's office. A few years after I first met the psychologist, when I was heading off to the middle school, the doctor had me redo a couple of the tests. She said it was to make sure the medicine they had me taking was working the right way. Again, the tests were easy. They were like video games and puzzles. I guess it made sense to make sure the medicine was working right. Especially since I'd rather not take it if I didn't have to.

Taking the tests,

Toby

IF YOU'VE TAKEN TESTS TO SEE IF YOU HAVE ADHD,
WHAT WERE THEY LIKE?

WHAT DID YOUR PARENTS OR THE DOCTOR SAY
ABOUT HOW YOU DID ON THE TESTS? IF THEY
DIDN'T TELL YOU, MAYBE YOU COULD ASK THEM
ABOUT WHAT THE TEST SAID.

KNOWING HOW YOU DID CAN HELP YOU BETTER
UNDERSTAND YOURSELF. WHAT DID THE TESTS
HELP YOU TO UNDERSTAND ABOUT HOW YOU DO
THINGS OR HOW YOU LEARN BEST?

THEY SAY IT'S ADHD...
(WHAT DO I DO WITH THAT?)

Dear Journal,

After I took all those tests, the doctor showed me how I did. She explained that I have Attention Deficit Hyperactivity Disorder, or for short, ADHD.

Not all Attention Deficit Hyperactivity Disorders are the same. My doctor explained that I have the "Inattentive Type." The tests said that I'm pretty smart (lots of kids with ADHD are). But, the tests showed that it takes me longer to do things than most kids. The tests showed a bunch of other stuff too, but that's all I feel like writing down. Finding out I have ADHD makes me feel like being a bit secretive or private about it.

So, now that there's a name for how and why I do stuff, what do I do with that? It's not like I won a medal I want to show off to the world. In fact, I'm not so sure I want anyone to know.

Mom and Dad say that some of the teachers might need to know because then they can help me learn my best. That makes sense, but I don't like it. I don't want to be different.

My mom's a teacher and she tried to make me feel better by explaining that every kid is different whether or not they have a name for how they are different. I really do want to do my best in school, so I guess it makes sense that some teachers should know.

I don't want my friends to know! The doctor says that's normal to not want to tell friends. Sometimes we are afraid they will make fun of us. The doctor said it's okay not to say anything. It's kind of like having allergies. My friends with allergies don't go around announcing "I am allergic to cats!" They don't say anything at all unless they want to or need to.

It's the same with ADHD. I don't have to tell my friends I have it unless I want or need to. I might need to if I spend the night at a friend's house and need help taking my medicine. (But even the moms or dads can work it out so none of my friends know, if I want.)

What do I do with all the information about having ADHD? The doctor says we should use the information to help me be my best. Knowing how I learn will help me get better grades in school. Knowing that it takes me longer to get things done will help my parents better understand me at home too! I guess we use the information to make life easier.

So, Journal, I have ADHD. I guess that's just part of who I am and how I do things. My family and I better understand how I tick... how my brain works, how I learn, why I do things the way I do. I can tell people who might need to know in order to help me be my best, or I can keep my ADHD private. It all depends. Best of all, with my parents' help, I get to choose who I tell and how I use the information to be my best!

Getting to choose what I do with my ADHD,
Toby

WHO EXPLAINED TO YOU THAT YOU HAVE ADHD?

- ☐ mom
- ☐ dad
- ☐ doctor
- ☐ somebody else

DID THEY TELL YOU...

- ☐ a little bit about ADHD
- ☐ just enough about ADHD
- ☐ way too much about ADHD

HOW DOES IT MAKE YOU FEEL NOW THAT YOU KNOW YOU HAVE THIS THING CALLED ADHD?

- ☐ better
- ☐ worse
- ☐ haven't thought about it

DO YOU THINK IT HELPS YOUR PARENTS BETTER UNDERSTAND YOU?

- ☐ yes
- ☐ no
- ☐ dunno

DIFFERENT KINDS OF ADHD

Dear Journal,

So, you've got cheese pizza, pepperoni pizza, even peanut butter pizza. (It's true! It's one of my favorites!) Well, just like there are different kinds of pizzas, there are different types of ADHD.

There's the "Flash Lightning" one where your motor is running fast and you are always on the go, wiggling, thinking, and doing things at a super fast speed. That's the Hyperactive Type of ADHD.

Then there's the "Day Dreaming Dude" one where you might seem spaced-out or day-dreamy to others who don't understand you. That's the Inattentive Type of ADHD.

Of course, just like nothing's ever black and white or this and that, neither is ADHD. Sometimes you can have a combo of both Hyperactive and Inattentive ADHD. That's me! But, I'm mostly the Inattentive Type.

Just like pizza, one type isn't really any better or worse than the other. It's just how it's made! Knowing what type of ADHD you have helps you and others better understand how and why you do things. For example, once we figured out that I have Inattentive ADHD, some things made a whole lot more sense. Like, I understood why I was always the last one to get ready to go to school in the morning. And my parents finally understood why I had so much homework every night. It was because I had trouble getting my work done during class and spent a lot of time looking out the window, watching the world outside!

The doctors could really explain to me and my parents how these little things in my brain called neurons take off and then have trouble getting to the spot they are supposed to go inside my head. Because they get a little lost...it takes longer for me to get the information in my brain where it needs to go quickly, and then I get lost too getting from my bed to my toothbrush!

It totally helped my teachers understand why it took me so much longer to get my projects done as well. Best of all, it helped me to realize that I'm not stupid or SLOW, I just do things differently and need strategies to help me.

Inattentive Type and peanut butter pizza lover,
Toby

WHAT TYPE OF ADHD DO YOU HAVE?

- ☐ Hyperactive
- ☐ Inattentive
- ☐ Combined (the super duper deluxe version)
- ☐ I'm not sure

HOW DOES THAT TYPE OF ADHD MAKE YOU DIFFERENT?

RECIPE

PEANUT BUTTER PIZZA

Ingredients:

- Frozen cheese pizza
- Jar of peanut butter
- Hungry stomach

Prepare the frozen pizza as directions say on the package. Remove the pizza and let it cool. Take a giant knife gobbed with peanut butter and gently spread it over the cooled cheese. Grab your slices before your sister does and EAT!

TO TELL OR NOT TO TELL...
THAT IS THE QUESTION

Dear Journal,

    Now I know that I have ADHD Inattentive Type. The doctors know. My parents, grandparents, and sister know. But should I tell anyone else? Do I have to tell anyone else? The doctor says it's up to me and my parents who we tell about my ADHD. Right now I don't feel like telling anybody. It makes me feel different...like there's something wrong with me.

??

    The doctor did a good job explaining that ADHD is not a disease, that there's nothing wrong with me. Instead, ADHD explains a little more about who I am and how my brain works. So who needs to know how my brain works? Maybe my teachers, I guess. It's their job to help me use my brain and learn all kinds of things. I suppose it would make sense to tell them about my ADHD....

One day in school, a teacher's assistant actually got mad at me because I was going too slowly on some classwork! She thought I was dorking around trying to go slowly because I didn't want to do the work! But I wasn't going slowly on purpose. It was just the way my brain was working. It took me longer than the other kids to read the paragraphs, find the answers in the book, and write them down on the worksheet.

I got an A on the assignment, but it just took me a lot longer to get it done. It didn't help to have her sitting there nagging me and making me feel dumb. She made it hard for me to focus and she made me feel like an idiot! If she had known about how my brain works, maybe she wouldn't have nagged me for going so slow. Then I wouldn't have felt so dumb.

I think it will be smart to have my parents help me tell the teachers who need to know. That way I can do my best in school. As for telling other people, like cousins or friends...I'm not sure if I'm ready to tell or not to tell yet. I'll leave it as a question for a while.

Telling just a few for now,

Toby

DO YOU TELL OTHERS YOU HAVE ADHD?

- ☐ yes
- ☐ no

IF YES, THEN WHO HAVE YOU TOLD AND WHY DID YOU TELL THEM?

- ☐ because you felt like it
- ☐ so they would better understand you
- ☐ because you think they have ADHD too
- ☐ for some other reason:

WHAT DID YOU TELL THEM ABOUT HAVING ADHD?

IS THERE ANYONE YOU HAVEN'T TOLD THAT YOU THINK SHOULD KNOW?

WHO?

WHAT'S KEEPING YOU FROM TELLING THEM?
- ☐ worried
- ☐ scared
- ☐ embarrassed
- ☐ just haven't gotten to it yet
- ☐ want your mom or dad to do it
- ☐ some other reason:

IS THERE ANYONE YOU **DON'T** WANT TO KNOW THAT YOU HAVE ADHD?

WHO?

Why?

I'M NOT THE ONLY ONE

Dear Journal,

This ADHD thing makes me feel different or weird. Sometimes I think that I am the only one in the world who has ADHD. My parents try to make me feel better by telling me all about famous people who have ADHD. Did you know that my favorite scientist, Albert Einstein, supposedly had ADHD? When I stop to think about it, it makes sense. His brain totally worked in a different way. That's what made him so amazing! Knowing that other people, like Einstein, have ADHD makes me feel less alone.

I'm not the only one with ADHD. In fact, my doctor told me that possibly one out of every ten kids has some type of ADHD. There are about 150 kids in my grade. Ah-ha! That means that there could be fifteen kids in my grade who have ADHD just like me. Get this, that means there could be about 200 kids in my school district with ADHD! I am NOT the only one!

Not the only one,

Toby

HAVE YOU EVER FELT LIKE YOU ARE THE ONLY PERSON ON THE PLANET WITH ADHD? WHY OR WHY NOT?

☐ yes

☐ no

HOW DOES THAT MAKE YOU FEEL?

HOW MANY KIDS DO YOU THINK HAVE ADHD IN YOUR GRADE? ____

Guess what! You can figure it out yourself. It won't be "for sure," but it will be pretty close! All you have to do is take the number of kids in your grade and divide that number by ten!

I have one hundred and fifty kids in my class. So I divide one hundred and fifty by ten. That equals about fifteen kids in my grade who probably have some type of ADHD!

$$150 \div 10 = 15$$

YOU DO IT! YOU WILL PROVE THAT YOU ARE NOT
ALONE!

$$\underline{} \div 10 = \underline{}$$

DO YOU KNOW OTHER PEOPLE WITH ADHD? IF SO,
HOW DOES KNOWING OTHER PEOPLE HELP YOU FEEL
LESS LIKE THE ONLY PERSON WITH ADHD?

MULTIPLE CHOICE...WHO HAS ADHD?
- ☐ Singer Justin Timberlake
- ☐ Actor Will Smith
- ☐ Walt Disney
- ☐ Athlete Michael Jordan

(The answer can be found on page 127 in the chapter
on Famous Peeps with ADHD!)

THE GIFT OF ADHD

Dear Journal,

I've heard people say that having ADHD can be a gift. My mom even has a book called something like "The Gift of ADHD." In my opinion, a gift is either something wrapped in paper with a bow on top or something good that happens. ADHD isn't really something good that happened to me. And it's certainly not something I'd ask for on my birthday. Don't get me wrong, ADHD isn't all bad, but it definitely isn't a gift!

If I had to find the gift in ADHD, I guess you could say that ADHD makes me a super thinker.

ADHD makes my mind run. I think and think and think. I do it all the time and sometimes I can't stop. I think up possible ways to cure cancer, or how to build robots. I dream up my own solutions for solving crime. Who knows, maybe someday I can make some of my THINKING actually happen!?!?!?

All this thinking, especially late at night, can cause problems. In school, my thinking gets me off the task I should be on sometimes. And then there's all the thinking I do while lying in bed at night. It makes it super hard for me to go to sleep! So, my parents did some thinking too and figured out a way to stop me from thinking late at night. They found a natural supplement called melatonin. (Melatonin is something our bodies already make. But, mine just doesn't make enough!) I take one pill each night, and it makes my brain stop spinning so I can fall asleep!

I guess having ADHD is kind of like being a new species because not everyone has it. Maybe

ADHD'rs will become the new super problem solvers of the future? That would make ADHD a gift!

Gifted in my own way,

Toby

DO YOU THINK HAVING ADHD IS A GIFT? WHY OR WHY NOT?

WHAT ABOUT HAVING ADHD MIGHT MAKE YOU SPECIAL? I AM...

- ☐ creative
- ☐ funny
- ☐ brave
- ☐ spontaneous
- ☐ fast
- ☐ laid back
- ☐ enthusiastic
- ☐ adventurous
- ☐ helpful
- ☐ hyperfocused
- ☐ inventive

- ☐ intelligent
- ☐ persistent
- ☐ energetic
- ☐ passionate
- ☐ other:

DRAW THE BEST GIFT IN THE WORLD THAT YOU WOULD LIKE TO GET SOMEDAY!

TODAY I AM MAD!

Dear Journal,

Today I am just mad! I get that way sometimes. I'll be just fine and then it's like a light switch gets flipped and I'm MAD!

I can get mad over the craziest things...like not wanting my tooth to fall out or flipping out of the stupid hammock. Everyone gets mad once in a while. Being mad is okay...it's how you choose to handle your mad that is important.

Sometimes, I get mad a lot and I get stuck being mad. First my fists start to clench. Then my arms get all tight and the anger just keeps rising. I've been so mad sometimes that I...(don't wanna talk about it).

I've worked with different people on turning my mad down. They teach me tricks to stay in control of my mad like counting down from ten, or breathing slowly. Their tricks are good ideas, but they don't always work. I'm me, Toby with a **Y,** and I've learned that I have to find my own way to do things sometimes.

I like to punch pillows when I get mad. I don't recommend feather pillows, though. One time I punched a fluffy feather pillow and it looked like a million chickens had been attacked by coyotes in my bedroom.

Everyone gets mad. That's pretty normal. But learning to control your mad and keep your cool can be hard.

Keeping my cool,

Toby

EVERYBODY GETS MAD NOW AND THEN. HOW OFTEN
DO YOU GET MAD?

☐ 1-3 times a day
☐ 1-3 times a week
☐ 1-3 times a month
☐ other: _____ times a _____

WHAT MAKES YOU MAD? (CHECK ALL THAT APPLY.)

☐ your mom (or dad) nagging you
☐ having homework or chores to do
☐ your brother or sister annoying you
☐ having to take a med
☐ having to get up early in the morning
☐ being told you have to practice your
   instrument
☐ other (you name it):

WHAT'S THE MADDEST YOU'VE EVER BEEN?

WHAT DO YOU DO TO CONTROL YOUR MAD?
(CHECK ALL THAT APPLY.)

☐ breathe deeply

☐ go outside to play

☐ go shoot hoops or play your favorite sport

☐ take a bathroom break (if in school)

☐ go to your room to chill

☐ close your eyes and pretend you're somewhere
   else (like snowboarding or swimming)

☐ go ride your bike

☐ go take a walk

☐ go talk to someone who keeps you calm

☐ text your friends

☐ write down how you feel in a journal

☐ other (fill in what works for you):

FINDING MY HAPPY

Dear Journal,

　　Today I headed to the hill to do a little snowboarding, and man, did I ever find my happy. It just really feels good to get out there and fly down the hill fast and hit the rails just right! When I hit a jump and catch air, I feel super free and get this rush of adrenaline that fills me with this total feeling of happy. I guess that happy feeling is really called a "natural high."

　　I get my natural highs boardin'. Snowboarding, skateboarding, wake boarding...anything with a board gives me that happy feeling.

Not everyone has to board to find their happy. Some of my friends find their happy by snowmobiling, going for a run, playing a game of hoops, going fishing, or even sailing a boat. It doesn't matter how you find your happy as long as you have a way to find it!

When I don't get a chance to do those things that give me that happy feeling, I can get really cranky. I can get in a mood that is just down and not any fun for others to be around.

When I'm in a bad mood, it causes other problems. Sometimes I can't focus to do my homework because of my mood. Other times, I get into fights with my sister... just because! But, if I had time to "find my happy" first, then I'm better at getting along with others and getting my homework done. I guess it's important to make time to "find my happy."

Hope you find your happy!

Toby

WHAT TYPES OF THINGS DO YOU LIKE TO DO THAT
HELP YOU "FIND YOUR HAPPY?"

HOW DO YOU FEEL WHEN YOU DON'T GET TO DO
THOSE THINGS?

HOW DO YOU FEEL WHEN YOU ARE BUSY DOING
THOSE THINGS THAT GIVE YOU THAT HAPPY,
NATURAL HIGH FEELING?

LET'S THINK BIG! IF YOU COULD PICK ANYTHING NEW THAT WOULD MAKE YOU HAPPY, WHAT WOULD IT BE?

YOU FILL IN THE BLANKS!

SPEND A MILLION DOLLARS ON:

TAKE A TRIP TO:

GET TICKETS TO:

LEARN HOW TO:

DID YOU TAKE YOUR MED???

Dear Journal,

Now that I'm a middle schooler, my parents are letting me take more control over the meds I take to help control my ADHD symptoms. Seems like all I hear now is... "Did you take your med?"

It's important to be responsible with medicines. I like the med I take now 'cause I can take it myself. Some meds are too dangerous, and parents really need to give it to you no matter how old you are. To be honest, my mom or dad still usually lays out the pills I take in the morning and at supper time. Even with reminders that help, I'm still learning to be independent about taking it before I hear, "Did you take your med?"

Ugggggggg! Sometimes I go to the counter to grab the med and between the time I take off and

get to the counter, I get sidetracked ...sometimes
it's the iPod I left charging on the kitchen table,
or maybe it's the science experiment stuff I dug out
yesterday and left out on the counter. Instead of
going right to the med and popping it in my mouth,
I end up poking at the moldy something I'm trying to
get to grow. Then I hear..."Did you take your med?"

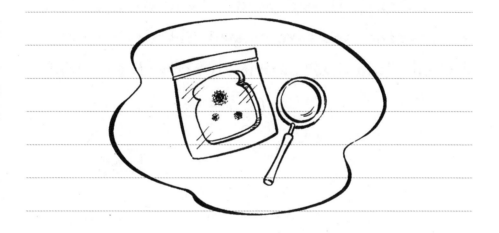

I really wish I didn't have to take a med or
have to be an independent rememberer! But...after
five years of trying to figure out what works best
for me, I know that taking the med is important.
Without taking the med, I won't just hear, "Did you
take your med?" I'll also hear:

- "Did you remember to finish your homework?"
- "Did you remember to meet your sister after school and walk with her home?"
- "Did you remember to pack your cold lunch?"
- "Did you remember to practice your guitar before you went out to skateboard?"

I guess I will work hard to build my independence and take my med. There's no doubt that one "Did you?" question is better than a ton!

Taking my meds,

Toby

IF YOU TAKE MEDS FOR ADHD, HOW DOES IT MAKE
YOU FEEL TO HAVE TO TAKE THEM?

I FEEL LIKE MY MEDICINE HELPS ME...
 ☐ all of the time
 ☐ some of the time
 ☐ never

HOW DO YOUR PARENTS HELP YOU TAKE YOUR MEDS
SO YOU CAN BE RESPONSIBLE TO DO IT ON YOUR
OWN SOMEDAY?

ROCK BRAIN

Dear Journal,

Sometimes I get what my family calls "rock brain." That means that I get stuck on an idea and I can't let it go. My brain is as hard as a rock!

I get rock brain at least once a day over something. Sometimes I have trouble making it go away, and then it causes trouble. Like the time I wanted chocolate chip cookie dough ice cream. My mind got set on getting some of that ice cream to my stomach, and my brain got as hard as a rock! Nothing was going to stop me. The problem was, we didn't have any chocolate chip cookie dough ice cream in the freezer, we were nowhere close to a grocery store, and it was after nine o'clock at night. Rock brain had hit!

I was about to melt down (have an obnoxious temper tantrum) all over ice cream. I know, it sounds a bit crazy to get all nuts just over ice cream. But, that's what rock brain does. It's like my brain gets locked up on that one thought or idea and I can't change it or make the thought go away.

My mom and dad tell me they have tricks to help me get out of rock brain. I can't believe they do, but who knows? They tell me they sometimes 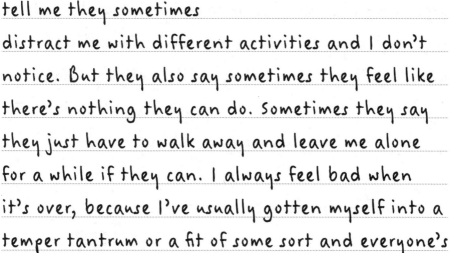 distract me with different activities and I don't notice. But they also say sometimes they feel like there's nothing they can do. Sometimes they say they just have to walk away and leave me alone for a while if they can. I always feel bad when it's over, because I've usually gotten myself into a temper tantrum or a fit of some sort and everyone's frustrated. Rock brain can be ugly and get me into trouble too!

I wish I could say I have my own tricks to get out of rock brain. But the truth is, it's called rock brain for a reason. It's hard and it's not going to change except over time, just like a rock when it gets worn down or tossed somewhere else, I guess. Rock brain just goes with the territory for some people with ADHD.

Rock brain can be frustrating...but it's also a sign that I have determination. Determination can be a great quality! For example, sometimes I'm practicing a great song on my drum set and I just can't get it right. Suddenly, rock brain will set in and I won't quit practicing until I get the song figured out. Perhaps someday rock brain will be a quality that helps me do great things!

Rockin' the rock brain,

Toby

WHAT KINDS OF THINGS MAKE YOU GET ROCK BRAIN?

HOW DO YOU GET OUT OF IT IF YOU NEED TO?

WHICH OF THESE TRICKS DO YOU THINK YOUR
FRIENDS OR FAMILY COULD USE TO HELP WHEN
YOU HAVE ROCK BRAIN?

☐ try to change the subject

☐ ask me to go do something different

☐ let me be and walk away and ignore the
situation

☐ offer me a piece of gum to get my body and
brain to loosen up

☐ other (name your own trick):

"FOR REAL" FRIENDS

Dear Journal,

    Remember how when I first found out that I have ADHD I didn't want to tell anyone? Well, since then, I've found out that real friends don't care if I have ADHD, just like friends don't care if you have allergies! Real friends don't care if you have crooked teeth or hat hair, and REAL FRIENDS won't care if you have ADHD. In fact, a real friend likes you for who you are, and having ADHD is part of who you are.

    Telling my friends was hard at first...it made me feel weird or different. But there was this one time that a friend spent the night at my cabin and he saw me take my meds. He didn't even say anything. Another time I had a friend over and when he saw me take my med, he said, "Hey, I take that same pill!" That sure surprised me. That's been the coolest part about letting some of my friends know that I have ADHD...I've been finding out that many of them have ADHD or something they have to take meds for too!

Once, I was snowboarding with a friend. I was feeling "superhero brave" practicing a trick on the rails. My mom hates that part of me having ADHD. Sometimes it means I can be a bit braver than I should be. The doctor has a real explanation about it...something about my frontal lobe being developmentally delayed. This means that I don't always think about the risks before I do certain things, like trying 360s on ice-packed snow!

Anyway, one time a friend of mine actually said, "You're lucky you have ADHD. It makes you a better boarder." I'm not so sure that's true, but I get what he was saying.

It was nice to hear a friend say something nice about my ADHD rather than tease me or make fun of me. Real friends see the good in a person and even the good in having ADHD!

A "for real" friend,

Toby

LIST YOUR "FOR REAL" FRIENDS.

WHAT DO YOU LIKE ABOUT THESE FRIENDS?

WHAT DO YOUR "FOR REAL" FRIENDS LIKE ABOUT YOU?

IF YOU HAVEN'T TOLD ANY FRIENDS YET, WHO WILL YOU TELL FIRST?

WHY?

IF YOU'VE ALREADY TOLD SOME "FOR REAL"
FRIENDS, WHY'D YOU TELL THEM FIRST?

WHAT DID THEY DO OR SAY WHEN YOU TOLD THEM?

I THINK MY EARS ARE PLUGGED

Dear Journal,

Today my parents got really frustrated with me. They told me to "go clean out my ears!" Sometimes I'm super focused on something, and I just don't realize that anything else is happening around me. Like one time, Dad was hollering for me to come fast with a towel because the toilet was overflowing! (Gross, I know, but stink happens.)

When I zone out, I think my ears are plugged! Who doesn't hear their dad hollering and their sister squealing? The truth is... sometimes I just have so much going on in my brain that I don't seem to hear.

On the outside, it looks like I don't care or like I don't want to listen. It's not that I don't care, I just really don't hear what they want me to because I am super focused on something else. My ears are usually plugged when I get super focused on a TV show, a video game, or something I'm doing on the computer.

I don't know why or how I get super focused doing those things...I just do. I kinda wish I could get that super focused in school when I should be getting work done, but that just doesn't happen.

Someday being super focused might come in handy on a big job when I'm an adult. Maybe someday I will have a job that will need me to zoom in on a computer project? Instead of getting tired, maybe my super focus will kick in and I'll be able to work until the job is done?

For now, I haven't found a good way to unplug my ears when I get super focused. It pretty much takes someone getting really up close in my face or unplugging what I'm plugged into! An occasional ear cleaner helps too!

Cleaning my ears out,

Toby

DO YOU HAVE A PROBLEM WITH SUPER FOCUSING TOO?
COMPLETE THE SENTENCE BELOW AND FIND OUT:

SOMETIMES I GET SO FOCUSED ON SOMETHING THAT
MY EARS ARE PLUGGED TO EVERYTHING ELSE
GOING ON AND...

- ☐ I miss my mouth when eating.
- ☐ I run into a wall while walking.
- ☐ I don't answer the teacher when he or she calls on me.
- ☐ I don't notice the fire alarm is going off because I forgot the pizza in the oven.
- ☐ Other (add your own):

WHEN ARE YOU MOST LIKELY TO HAVE "PLUGGED
EARS" AND BE CLUELESS ABOUT WHAT'S GOING ON
AROUND YOU?

ARE THERE ANY TRICKS THAT HELP YOU SNAP OUT
OF THAT SUPER FOCUS? WHAT ARE THEY?

MAGNET MIND

Dear Journal,

Have you ever played with a really big magnet and lots of little pieces of metal like paper clips? It's a lot of fun to explore and see how many paper clips you can get to cling to a giant magnet.

Well, in math today my brain was just like a giant magnet. I had all kinds of "thinks" clinging to my brain. Only problem was, my brain was supposed to be focused on the smiling math teacher up front who was trying to explain how to solve the challenging algebra problem.

You know that push-away feeling you get when you put the opposite ends of two magnets together? That's how my brain felt about the math lesson. I just couldn't focus. It wasn't interesting and I had too many other thoughts clinging to my brain. I was busy thinking about how I had to hurry to ski team practice right after school. I couldn't stop worrying about the science test I had to take after lunch. I was wondering what was for lunch. And, I certainly couldn't avoid thinking about all the dandruff flaking off the head of the kid sitting in front of me, making little dandruff-snow piles on his shoulder.

I had MAGNET MIND in math!!! Cling, cling, cling!

My mom's been reading. She reads a lot! She showed me this article about how people are saying ADHD is sorta misnamed in a way. You see, it's called Attention Deficit Hyperactivity Disorder. But ADHD'rs don't really have a **deficit** of attention. They just can't **focus** their attention.

According to an online dictionary, **deficit** means: an amount that is less than it should be.

I don't think that's the best way to describe my brain. I had lots of thoughts going on in my head that I was paying attention to! I just couldn't zoom in and pay attention to just the math lesson. My brain was like a giant magnet with lots of paper clips clinging to it! I had my attention divided between too many thoughts.

I wasn't able to focus my attention like the other kids, and that became a problem in class. There stood that smiling teacher with a loud booming voice explaining how to solve for x. But even with her voice thundering, I couldn't keep my attention on just her and my math. Of course she called on me!

There I sat with that sick, embarrassed feeling on the inside and that zoned-out look on the outside. She was probably thinking, "What a blockhead. There's nothing going on inside that kid's brain."

But really, I'm not a blockhead. No way! There's lots going on inside my brain. There's sometimes too much going on up in there that I can't focus my attention the way I need to. Instead...I'm a magnet mind!

Magnet mind,

Toby

IN CLASS IT'S...

☐ easy to stay focused on the teacher

☐ hard to stay focused on the teacher

☐ somewhere in between

WHAT CLASS IS THE EASIEST TO KEEP YOUR ATTENTION ZOOMED IN?

WHAT CLASS IS THE HARDEST TO KEEP YOUR ATTENTION ZOOMED IN?

WHAT DO YOU SAY WHEN A TEACHER CALLS ON YOU
AND YOU WEREN'T ZOOMED IN?

- ☐ Sorry, I didn't hear you.
- ☐ Uh...I don't know.
- ☐ I need more time to think about it.
- ☐ I think "so and so" has a better answer—let them explain.
- ☐ Choose your own way to respond:

WHAT WOULD YOU PICK UP WITH A GIANT MAGNET
IF YOU COULD CHOOSE?

- ☐ paper clips
- ☐ car keys (to a really cool Mustang)
- ☐ staples off the classroom floor
- ☐ a "no math homework" pass
- ☐ gold coins
- ☐ buried treasure on the beach
- ☐ you choose:

TICS AREN'T JUST BROWN BUGS

Dear Journal,

Did you know that tics aren't just brown bugs? It's true! When I was little, I used to have this habit of pulling on my lower lip...a lot. Nobody thought very much of it until a couple of years later when I stopped pulling on my lip and started blinking my eyes for no real reason. I couldn't explain why I did it, I just did. The more someone brought it up, the worse it got.

On a regular visit to the doctor, we asked about my blinking. The doctor explained that I have tics... and no, they are not the brown bugs (ticks) that you get after playing out in the woods or out in your fort! These tics are little habits that my body does that I can't control.

I've had different tics over the years. Like I said, it started as pulling on my lip. Then it went to blinking my eyes. The summer before I started middle school, my tic turned into a little sound that would just pop out of my mouth really quiet-like. My mom didn't even notice it until my dad brought it up. They were worried that if that tic kept going, I might get picked on in school. Thankfully, it was such a quiet sound from my voice nobody noticed. But just in case, I practiced how I would explain why I did it. It's better that teachers and friends understand why some things happen rather than just ignore it and let them think that I do it on purpose or to be a ninny.

Thankfully, the tic in my voice didn't last long. Instead, it moved to tugging on my ear. My parents

used to get on me and try to help me stop my tics.
I'd just get frustrated because no matter how hard
I'd try, it was an impulse that just took over and
happened. I couldn't control it.

Finally, after we all met with my therapist
one day, she taught my mom and dad that I really
couldn't stop my tics! It's true...she told us that you
can try to control them or change them a little, but
you can't make them stop. There's just something about
the way my brain is hooked up that doesn't let it stop.

The good news is that I most likely won't have
to live with these tics forever. They told me that they
usually hit their worst when a kid is ten to twelve
years old and then might gradually go away forever.
I hope so. My tics aren't very noticeable... so it's
really no big deal. In fact, it would be worse to be
covered with the tics that are the brown bugs!

Tic'n,

Toby

76

DO YOU HAVE TICS?

IF YOU DO, HOW DO YOU HANDLE THEM?

DO KIDS EVER NOTICE OR TEASE YOU?

HERE'S A LIST OF IDEAS TO HELP OTHERS
UNDERSTAND SO THEY DON'T TEASE. CHECK THE
ONES THAT YOU THINK YOU MIGHT USE.

- ☐ Be assertive and just tell them about your tic.
- ☐ Use humor and find a way to make your tic something special or fun about you.
- ☐ Have your teacher explain it during health class.
- ☐ Ask your parent to explain it to the parent of the kid who's teasing you.
- ☐ Other (What are your own ideas?):

SHE MADE ME DO IT

Dear Journal,

I really wanted this app for my iPod today. I know I'm not supposed to just buy apps without permission first. I just couldn't help myself. I didn't want to wait for Mom to get home, and Dad didn't know how to do it. Yep, so I did it anyway.

It's a great app and my sister and I were having tons of fun playing it when my mom got home. Of course my big mouth little sister had to go and tell mom about the cool new app we were playing... and then the trouble started! She made me do it! Well, not really, but that's what I told my mom.

I know, she really didn't make me do it, but it's always easier to blame someone else for my own mistake.

Sometimes, there's this part of my brain that just goes nuts when I know I'm going to be in trouble. That little voice in my head is there saying...don't pass the blame...but I do anyway! It's just like a burp that belches out before I can stop it! I should know better...because the truth always comes out and then I'm in even bigger trouble. I wish I could just slow my brain down and stop the blaming burp before it comes out!

Oh well, at least I have a great little sister to pass the blame onto! I am sorry it happens. I usually try to make it up to her somehow.

Trying to stop the blaming burp,

Toby

YOU PROBABLY BLAME OTHERS WHEN THINGS GO WRONG. TELL THE TRUTH. HAVE YOU EVER BEEN TEMPTED TO BLAME SOMEONE ELSE IN ANY OF THESE SITUATIONS?

- ☐ when something got broken
- ☐ when you forgot to do your homework
- ☐ when you were late getting somewhere (like school or basketball practice)
- ☐ when you forgot to do a chore
- ☐ when you forgot to flush the toilet
- ☐ when you ate all the ice cream, drank all the OJ, etc.
- ☐ when you forgot to feed the family pet
- ☐ when you ran over the shrub/flowers with the lawn mower
- ☐ other (add your own examples):

HOW DO YOU FEEL AFTER YOU BLAME SOMEONE
ELSE FOR YOUR OWN MISTAKE?

HOW DO YOU TRY TO FIX IT?

IS THERE A WAY YOU CAN THINK OF TO STOP
A BLAMING BURP FROM POPPING OUT OF YOUR
MOUTH?

MY "GO BUTTON" IS BROKEN

Dear Journal,

My mom says I have a "go button" and that it's broken. This morning we were all supposed to be getting ready to go to the science museum for a fun family day. We wanted to take off early so we could have plenty of time to explore and catch the cool Omni-Max movie on undersea treasures. I was really pumped about going! But I guess my go button was broken.

Dad kept reminding, "Go eat some breakfast." Mom kept saying, "Get your socks and shoes on." And anytime I wanted in the bathroom, my sister was hogging it! Pretty soon everyone had their jackets on and I was still sitting on the couch, no socks or shoes on, with a full plate of waffles that I hadn't even started eating yet.

I don't know what my go button is, but I guess you could say it seems to be broken sometimes! It's just really hard for me to GO! Sometimes, I start heading to the bathroom to brush my teeth so we can get going somewhere, and between the kitchen and the bathroom I get lost. Well, not really, but I get busy doing something like gathering my **Popular Science** magazines to take along on the car ride.

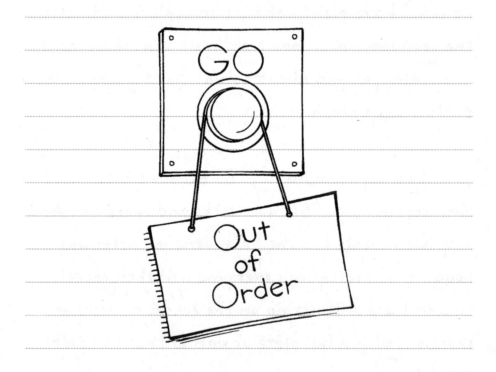

My mom and dad sometimes set the timer on the oven to help me keep track of how much time I have...but that can stress me out! I'm getting used to the timer, though...Some days it helps, some days not so much.

I wish there was a magic tool to fix my go button. I don't want to have a broken go button. But until I can find a way to "fix" it, I'll keep trying to find different ways to help me GO...like using the timer, or making a list of TO DO's, or turning it into a game of some sort.

Working with a broken "go button,"

Toby

DO YOU HAVE A BROKEN "GO BUTTON"? BROKEN "GO BUTTONS" ARE PRETTY NORMAL FOR KIDS WITH THE INATTENTIVE TYPE ADHD.

☐ yes
☐ no

IF YOU DON'T HAVE A BROKEN "GO BUTTON," DO YOU HAVE A BROKEN "STOP BUTTON"?

In other words, does your motor go too fast so you don't stop to think before you do things? Broken "stop buttons" are pretty normal for kids with the Hyperactive Type ADHD.

☐ yes
☐ no

WHAT PROBLEMS DOES IT CAUSE IF YOU TAKE A LONG TIME GETTING READY OR STARTING ON SOMETHING YOU NEED TO DO?

WHAT KINDS OF TRICKS COULD YOU OR YOUR
PARENTS USE TO HELP YOU GET GOING?
HERE ARE SOME IDEAS...

- ☐ Try to race the timer on the stove.
- ☐ Use a cool visual timer app on an iPad or iPod.
- ☐ Put your alarm clock on the other side of the room in the morning so you have to get up and go across the room to turn it off (be sure to set it on a loud obnoxious ring).
- ☐ Use the "this first and then that" trick. For example, get your math done first and then you can go play the video game you're dying to play.
- ☐ Make a plan with your teacher and parents that rewards a working "go button." Like, if you get going on your work in class within a minute or two of start time, then you only have to do eight problems instead of ten.
- ☐ Keep it simple...have only one choice for breakfast in the morning, or make sure your outfit is picked out and ready to jump into

in the morning so you don't sit and spin, wondering what to eat or wear.

☐ Give yourself a payoff! For example, practice your instrument for fifteen minutes and then you can have that healthy treat you want to eat! (Okay, maybe sometimes it's not even all that healthy!)

HAY-WIRED WITH HOMEWORK

Dear Journal,

    I HATE HOMEWORK! Did I shout that out loud enough? Yep, it's true. The deal is, I have a hard time staying focused in school. Because of that, I don't get very much done during class. That means...MORE HOMEWORK! I get my regular homework and then all the stuff I didn't get done during the school day.

    By the time I get home, I am so overwhelmed by all the work that the wires in my brain get hay-wired! Then, because my brain is going berserk, I can't even get going on my homework. I sit there MAD!

When the wires in my brain are hot and hay-wired, I gotta let them cool down before I can get anything done. A good snack and time out on my bike first often help me get into a better mood to tackle my homework.

Then, I need to get organized! I make a "TO DO" list. I try to think of all the things I need to get done. My mom or dad often helps me decide what I should do first. Sometimes I'd rather do my science first (even though it's not due for three days) instead of my math because science can be fun. I get to watch frog dissections and stuff like that on the computer... That's way more fun than trying to divide fractions without a calculator!

Anyway, I get my "TO DO" list done and prioritize what I should do first. Then, I open my backpack and only take out the one thing I'm going to focus on first. See, if I take it all out and put it on the table, it looks like a mountain and there goes my brain again...hay-wired!

Once I get going, I don't stop very much. I can really get my wires whipping and my homework done! I just wish I wouldn't get so overwhelmed and let my wires get hay-wired in the first place.

Trying to rewire my brain,

Toby

PUT AN **X** WHERE YOU LAND WHEN IT COMES TO
HOW YOU FEEL ABOUT HOMEWORK:

homework stinks   homework happens   homework is exciting

WHEN YOU HAVE HOMEWORK, YOU...
- ☐ get it done right away
- ☐ go hang out a bit and then do it later
- ☐ wait until the last minute to start it
- ☐ hide it so you don't have to do it
- ☐ get so overwhelmed by it that you have a
  meltdown

WHAT HOMEWORK IS ACTUALLY KINDA FUN TO DO? (I
LIKE TO DO HOMEWORK THAT IS ON THE COMPUTER!)

WHAT'S THE WORST HOMEWORK YOU HAVE TO DO?

WHAT STRATEGIES DO YOU HAVE THAT HELP YOU
GET YOUR HOMEWORK DONE?

☐ have a set place and time to do your
homework every night

☐ use the "this and then that" strategy (for
example, do math first and then ride your
bike)

☐ break the homework down into small chunks
to do over the evening

☐ go outside and get some fresh air and free
time before you get started

☐ other (list your own strategies):

THERE'S A VOLCANO IN MY LOCKER

Dear Journal,

Some days I swear there is a volcano in my locker. It usually explodes when I need to get to a class in a hurry and I can't find the right folder. Pretty soon there's an eruption...Papers are everywhere, markers are spilling from the top shelf down to the bottom, the straps from my backpack hang out and I can't get the locker closed and keep the volcano from spilling out into the hall!

I know having ADHD can wreak havoc on my ability to keep things together. I'm always being told, "You need to work on staying organized." I know, I know, I know...but trying to be organized doesn't make the volcano go away. Using some organizational tricks can help me keep the volcano from exploding once in a while, though.

Here are some of the things I do to try and stay organized...

- Use color-coded notebooks and folders for each class...like, math is blue!
- Use a weekly agenda to keep track of assignments.
- Use sticky notes to put a "TO DO" on the cover of my assignment books so they are right there looking at me!

- Use some kind of a holder or bucket to keep all my pens and pencils in one spot and easy to grab fast.
- Keep a plastic grocery bag hanging inside my locker to toss any garbage or no-longer-needed papers into it right away (otherwise they tend to pile up at the bottom of my locker, turning the volcano into a volcanic mountain).

Okay, so I have these tricks to use, but that doesn't always mean that my papers make it into the folders, or the pens get put back in the holder, and yeah, lots of times I'm outta sticky notes to put my TO DO's on the top of my assignment books. But, each day is a new day, and how many times the volcano explodes inside my locker changes...just like I'm changing each and every day as I figure out what works best for me and this ADHD.

Keeping a lid on the volcanoes,

Toby

DO YOU HAVE A VOLCANO THAT EXPLODES IN YOUR LOCKER OR DESK SOMETIMES? WHAT MAKES IT SOOOOOOO MESSY THAT A VOLCANO EXPLODES?

I ONCE FOUND A ROTTING APPLE IN MY LOCKER THAT HAD TURNED BLACK! WHAT'S THE NASTIEST THING YOU EVER FOUND IN YOUR LOCKER OR DESK?

ARE THERE ANY ORGANIZATIONAL TRICKS THAT YOU USE THAT HELP?
WHICH WORK?

WHICH DON'T AND WHY?

WHO COULD YOU ASK TO HELP YOU COME UP WITH SOME IDEAS TO KEEP A LID ON THE VOLCANO IN YOUR DESK OR LOCKER?

COOL COUNSELORS

Dear Journal,

School can get a bit crazy sometimes. I really do like going to school, seeing my friends, and learning about some cool stuff like the Oregon Trail and fungi! But sometimes I have a crazy problem and I'm too nervous to try and solve it by myself. I'm pretty lucky to have a Cool Counselor to help me when I'm too worried to solve a problem by myself.

Schools sometimes have these adults called counselors who are there to help kids solve their problems. They aren't like teachers in the classroom—they're more like adult friends who have time to help you and talk about things and problems. My counselor has this little room off of the office and I can pretty much go see her anytime I need to. Of course, sometimes she knows I need her before I do, and she calls for me to come for a chat....

One time I had this science teacher who put tons of notes up on the board about single-celled creatures. We were supposed to copy all the notes down while he talked about it. But, I was so into what he was saying that I didn't get all the notes down before he switched the page. The teacher kept going, and I kept falling further behind. Trouble was, I needed those notes for a quiz he was going to give us the next day. I wanted to do well on the quiz, but I needed the notes and I was too worried to figure out how to solve the problem.

When I got home that night, I was a wreck. My mom asked why I didn't just ask the teacher for more time to write the notes down...Well, I didn't want to bug him. And, there's just never enough time! I was really upset. I just knew I was going to fail the quiz, and I like doing well in school.

After my mom and dad helped me calm down, we worked together on an email to my Cool Counselor. Mom knew that she'd be able to check in with me and help me solve this problem. In school the next day, my counselor and I worked together to figure out how to talk to the teacher and explain my situation. I was still worried, but I knew that she'd help me make this epic problem go away. She did!

These kinds of problems used to happen to me a lot at first in middle school. But the more I worked with my Cool Counselor, the more ways she showed me to solve problems and work things out for myself.

I still get into sticky spots sometimes, but now I'm more likely to go and talk to the teacher on my own to solve the problem. Mom and Dad notice that I'm much more independent now in school...but we

all agree that it's nice to have my Cool Counselor
to call on if I ever need help with a problem, or just
want to chat!

Keeping it cool with a counselor,
Toby

DOES YOUR SCHOOL HAVE A COUNSELOR?

☐ yes

☐ no

WHAT'S YOUR GUIDANCE COUNSELOR'S NAME?

DO YOU EVER GET TO CHAT WITH THE COUNSELOR?
IF SO, WHAT THINGS DOES THE COUNSELOR HELP
YOU WITH?

WHAT WOULD IT BE LIKE IF YOU DIDN'T HAVE
YOUR COUNSELOR'S HELP?

COUNSELORS ARE THERE TO HELP KIDS!

If you'd like to talk to the one in your school, ask your mom or dad to help you connect with him or her. Or ask a teacher you like about talking to the counselor. You could also be brave and just knock on the counselor's door!

IF YOU HAVEN'T MET WITH A COUNSELOR, WHAT MIGHT YOU LIKE TO TALK TO ONE ABOUT? WHAT WOULD YOU LIKE HELP WITH SOMETIMES?

MEDS...DO I HAVE TO?

Dear Journal,

Meds...they are a daily "TO DO!" There are some kids who can find ways to control their ADHD without meds. I wish I was one of those kids, but for now, I'm not!

When I was younger I HATED having to take my meds, and I'd always ask...DO I HAVE TO??? It was like something my mom and dad made me do. Doctors give me certain meds to help me focus better. The teachers and my parents say they notice a difference when I take them, so it's IMPORTANT to take my meds.

I didn't think they did any good. Then, there was this morning that was super busy, and we all forgot about my med. Oh boy, was that a day! In that one day...I forgot my chapter book at home, I missed my band lesson, and I couldn't focus during a math test and ended up bombing it. Worst of all, I couldn't get my backpack stuffed fast enough and I missed the bus home! That day taught me that even though I don't feel like I need my meds, if I don't take them, things just don't go as well!

I've tried a bunch of different meds. Between my doctor, my parents, my teachers, and ME, we try to figure out if the meds work the right way. Some meds I took didn't seem to make my focus any better in school. Another med I took made it too hard for me to eat anything and I was getting way too skinny. That was not cool. It made me feel worse about myself instead of better. Then, there was this one med that made me into a zombie.

I know, zombies can be cool, but that's only if they are in books or movies. You really don't want to be one. Trust me!

It took some time (like a couple of years) to figure out the best med for me. And even now that we have one that seems to work well, we're always having to change how much I take because of how fast I am growing.

My mom and dad used to have to give me my med. Now that I'm getting older, they are letting me be in charge of my meds (with their help, of course). It's kinda nice to start to be responsible for myself.

Of course, I still wish I didn't have to take my meds...it's a pain and it just makes me feel different than everybody else. But, I guess as I get older, I'm getting wiser and know that YES...I have to! That is, if I want to remember to take my chapter book to school, get to my band lesson on time, ace the math test, and pack my backpack fast enough so I don't miss the bus!!!

Someday, I hope I won't need a med. I've even talked with my parents and the doctor about maybe someday trying to go without. That way we could see if I've gone through any changes that might make it possible to use strategies and diet instead of meds. My parents say it would have to be during the summer so I don't have to worry about schoolwork. That makes sense to me, I guess. I hear it's possible for some people with ADHD to learn strategies and grow enough to live without meds. I don't know if that will be me...too early to tell. But, I can hope!

Takin' my med for now,

Toby

DO YOU TAKE MEDS FOR ADHD?

☐ yes

☐ no

IF YES...HOW DO YOU KNOW THEY HELP YOU?

WHAT DO YOU THINK WOULD HAPPEN IF YOU
DIDN'T TAKE YOUR MED?

WOULD IT BE WORTH IT? WHY?

DO YOU EVER HAVE SIDE EFFECTS? (CHECK THE
ONES THAT BEST FIT YOU.)

☐ Sometimes they make me feel like a zombie.

☐ Sometimes they make me feel like I'm a
speeding bullet.

☐ I don't notice anything different.

☐ They make me grouchy.

☐ They make my stomach feel full and I don't
eat very much.

☐ They make me spin at night and it's hard to
fall asleep.

☐ Other (you fill in the blank):

A THERA-HUH?
SEEING A THERAPIST

Dear Journal,

I don't like talking to many people about having ADHD. It's really kind of a private thing. Sometimes I feel too embarrassed to talk about having ADHD. I'm getting better about talking about it with friends, and I know I can always talk to my family...but I don't always want to talk to them! So, I'm really glad I have a special person to talk to. That person is a THERAPIST.

When the doctor first told me I should see a therapist, I was like "What? A thera-HUH?" I hate feeling different and when the doctor said I should go see a therapist, that's exactly how I felt... DIFFERENT!

But guess what? LOTS of kids see a therapist. In one article my mom read (she really reads too much!), over 2.7 million kids were seeing a therapist for their ADHD. And that was way back in 2007! I guess if I'm one out of over 2.7 million kids, then I'm not so different for seeing a therapist!

Therapists are like doctors that you go chat with. My therapist's name is Dr. Susan, and I'm cool about talking to her about my ADHD.

Dr. Susan is super nice! Sometimes we talk. Sometimes we play games or even draw. No matter what, she always makes me feel okay about being me!

Dr. Susan has helped me come up with ideas on how to push my worries away. She's let me tell her about how mad I can get. We've even talked about how my mom and dad can frustrate me...get on my nerves...or try to control everything. No matter what, I can trust her. What I say to Dr. Susan stays with Dr. Susan! It's really cool to have someone like her that I can talk to and trust.

Not every therapist is a Dr. Susan, though. For a while, we tried a few different therapists because Dr. Susan is a really long drive from where we live. We thought it would be easier if I didn't have to miss school to see the therapist. That was a mistake!

One of the other therapists we tried didn't seem to really listen to me (or my mom and dad).

One week I told her about a worry I had and she had me do a breathing thing to try and push the worry away. We tried to tell her that it didn't work, but the next week we kept practicing the same activity. I swear this other therapist made me practice the same breathing technique for a month! Not only was I stuck with that worry I had...but I was getting mad too!

I guess we learned that not every therapist is a good fit. You gotta find the one you like and trust. The therapist should help you solve problems and really listen to you. And no matter what, it should be someone you don't mind going to see. A therapist should make you feel good about being you.

Off to the thera-pssst,
(I have something to talk about.)

Toby

DO YOU GO TO A THERAPIST?

☐ yes

☐ no

IF SO, WHAT KINDS OF THINGS DOES YOUR THERAPIST HELP YOU WITH (BEING MAD, WORRIES, GETTING SCHOOL WORK DONE, GETTING ALONG WITH OTHERS...)?

WHAT ARE YOUR FAVORITE ACTIVITIES YOU DO WITH YOUR THERAPIST AND WHY?

IF YOU DON'T SEE A THERAPIST, WHAT WOULD YOU
WANT TO TELL ONE THAT YOU MIGHT NOT WANT TO
TALK ABOUT WITH YOUR PARENTS OR FRIENDS?
Remember, a therapist is like a special friend you can
really talk to...so what would you wanna talk about?

HOW LONG DOES ADHD LAST?

Dear Journal,

Every time I go to the doctor, and that's about every three months, they always ask, "Do you have any questions?" Yes, I do, and it's always the same question: "When will this ADHD go away?" I know I'll get the same answer each time, but I ask anyway.

The doctor always says, "You never know! It could be like the freckle on your cheek and stay with you forever, or it could

June 2030						
Su	Mo	Tu	We	Th	Fr	Sa
	1	2	3	4	5	6
7	8	9	10	11	12	13
14	15	16	17			
21	22	23	24			
28	29	30				

May 2099						
Su	Mo	Tu	We	Th	Fr	Sa
					1	2	3
4	5	6	7	8	9	10
11	12	13	14	15	16	17
18	19	20	21	22	23	24
25	26	27	28	29	30	31

go away any day as you get older and your brain continues to develop."

You see, as you grow, so does your brain. The doctor says that the part of my brain that makes me have ADHD might grow a lot or a little. It's kind of like how tall you might grow! Nobody knows how tall you'll be.

If that part of my brain grows just a little, I might always want to use medicine to help me control my ADHD symptoms. Or, I might grow enough that I can succeed at a job or in college someday if I just use certain strategies. If the part of my brain that causes the ADHD symptoms develops a lot, it's even possible that all the things that make me ADHD right now will go away!

Of course, I hope it goes away, but there's no way to know what will happen, just like there's no way to know if I'll grow to be 5' 9" or 6' 2"! But,

I'm pretty sure there's a good chance that I'll be somewhere between 5' 9" and 6' 2"! That's probably what I can count on with my ADHD too...ending up somewhere in between!

Somewhere between,

Toby

I HOPE I "OUTGROW" MY ADHD. DO YOU HOPE
YOU'LL OUTGROW YOURS? WHY OR WHY NOT?

IF YOU HAVE ADHD FOREVER, HOW MIGHT THAT
AFFECT YOU? CHECK OFF WHAT MIGHT HAPPEN
TO YOU.

- ☐ I'll become a superstar in my future job.
- ☐ I might have trouble sticking with a career.
- ☐ I will have many amazing adventures.
- ☐ It might be a challenge to get through college, so if I want to go to college, I'll need a plan to succeed.
- ☐ I might invent some incredible things.
- ☐ I might lose my car keys a lot (when I'm old enough to buy my dream car).
- ☐ I might move to lots of different places (it's hard to stay still).

☐ I'll make lots of friends doing the things I love (like snowboarding or making music).

☐ I'll find (or even invent) apps that will help me be super organized and on time.

☐ I will need a job that fits the way I'm wired, and that job might be...

FAST FACTS ABOUT ADHD

Dear Journal,

    I'm still learning all about ADHD. One day I was so full of questions that my dad pulled up a website called "Facts about ADHD" (www.cdc.gov/ncbddd/adhd). He had me just read some fast facts. Here's what I learned:

- ADHD is REAL and one of the most common neurobehavioral disorders for children.
- Neurobehavioral means having to do with the way the brain affects emotion, behavior, and learning.
- Children with ADHD have trouble paying attention.
- Kids with ADHD may be impulsive—meaning they may speak or act without thinking.
- ADHD kids might forget to do things or lose objects.

- Children with ADHD might wiggle a lot.
- Kids with ADHD might not seem to listen (notice the word **seem**).
- Children with ADHD might be easily distracted.
- There are three different types of ADHD: Predominantly Inattentive Type, Predominantly Hyperactive-Impulsive Type, and Combined Type.
- Scientists are still studying why some kids have ADHD. The cause is still unknown!
- Some scientists have research that shows that genetics may play an important part in why some kids get ADHD. In other words, it seems to run in the family. (Again, notice the word **seems**.)
- Other possible causes scientists have studied include: brain injury, exposures to harmful things in the environment like lead, alcohol or tobacco use during pregnancy, or being born prematurely.

- Research does not support the opinion that kids get ADHD by eating too much sugar, watching too much TV, or coming from poor families.
- Some people still call the condition ADD, but the most current and correct name is ADHD followed by which type you have.
- ADHD can be treated with medication, behavioral therapy, or both. Some people have been able to treat it with diet as well.
- How ADHD is treated depends on the kid, and every kid is different.

Still learning,

Toby

WHAT OTHER FACTS CAN YOU ADD TO MY LIST OF
"FAST FACTS ABOUT ADHD?"

THERE'S SO MUCH TO LEARN ABOUT ADHD THAT
I ALWAYS SEEM TO HAVE QUESTIONS. WHAT
QUESTIONS DO YOU HAVE ABOUT ADHD?

FAMOUS PEEPS WITH ADHD

Dear Journal,

Did you know that there are famous people who have ADHD? My dad came home from work today with a cool list of all these amazing people who have ADHD! I was so surprised! The list had some of my favorite actors, musicians, and even people that changed the world. I told you ADHD'rs might be a new species and the future problem solvers for our planet! Check out this list of some of my favorite peeps with ADHD:

(Disclaimer Alert...According to our research, this list should be accurate...but you know how that goes! You just can't always trust all the resources out there online. One of my favorite TV personalities is Ellen DeGeneres. I tried to find out if she is a fellow ADHD'r...some sites say YES...

- Albert Einstein - physicist/inventor (He didn't even start talking until he was 4 years old!)
- Whoopi Goldberg - comedian/actor
- Justin Timberlake - singer/actor
- Howie Mandel - comedian/actor/game show host
- Michael Jordan - NBA basketball player
- Will Smith - actor/singer
- Karina Smirnoff - dancer
- Bill Cosby - comedian/actor
- John Lennon - singer
- Babe Ruth - baseball player
- Bill Gates - founder of Microsoft

some say NO. There's really no way to know unless you talk to these real people face to face. Wouldn't that be cool to ask Ellen or Albert Einstein face to face? So, like I said... I hope our research tells the truth. But the truth is hard to find. If I made a mistake... I'm SORRY!)

- Walt Disney - cartoonist/creator of everything Disney (He got fired from a job because they thought he didn't have any good ideas!)
- Benjamin Franklin - inventor and the person on the $100 bill

- Ludwig van Beethoven - music composer
- Michael Phelps - Olympic swimmer
- Solange Knowles - singer
- Jim Carrey - comedian/actor
- Leonardo da Vinci - Italian inventor/artist
- Thomas Edison - inventor (His teachers said he was too dumb to learn anything!)
- Henry Ford - inventor of the Ford automobile assembly line

- Galileo - mathematician/astronomer
- Milton Hershey — chocolate candy creator
- Magic Johnson - NBA basketball player
- Abraham Lincoln — 16th president of the USA
- Henry Winkler - actor/author (He's written the Hank Zipzer stories about a kid with ADHD!)

My dad found all these people listed on a website called **ADHD and More** (adhdandmore. blogspot.com 2009). There were so many names on just this one list that I was overwhelmed! Who would have thought that an American president would have ADHD? ADHD'rs can do ANYTHING!!!

A not-so-famous ADHD peep,

Toby

WHAT FAMOUS ADHD'RS DO YOU KNOW OF?

IF YOU COULD GROW UP TO BE A FAMOUS ADHD'R,
WHAT WOULD YOU BE?

NUMBER IN ORDER FROM MOST IMPORTANT TO
LEAST IMPORTANT TO YOU...

☐ money
☐ "for real" friends
☐ fame
☐ hobbies that help you find your "happy"
☐ family
☐ cool car

FINAL LETTER TO THE READER: STRETCHING THE TRUTH

Dear Reader,

Okay, sometimes I don't tell the full truth. Sometimes I take the truth and stretch it! It's fun using my imagination. It makes things more interesting.

So, if you were to ask me if EVERY WORD in this journal is the truth...I'd have to say both YES and NO. See, I sometimes stretched the truth or used my imagination a bit here and there.

Everything I put down in this journal really did happen in one way or another...I just maybe added a little twist now and then. My brain really does get hay-wired over homework. I really do have a Cool Counselor I can chat with and get help from in solving problems at school. I really do pass the blame off on my sister now and then. I just might not have gotten behind on notes about one-celled creatures...it might have been notes on something like food chains instead! Face it, one-celled creatures are more interesting than food chains.

Go ahead and try to figure out the parts that I've stretched or added a bit of imagination to. It's part of the fun! But no matter what, I've shared a lot of real stuff about me...a real kid with ADHD. I hope that by sharing my journal with you, I've helped you see that being a real kid with ADHD is normal, and not. And I really do believe that we are a new species that will be this world's future problem solvers! Here's to being real and having ADHD!

Your friend,

Toby

P.S. Wanna chat for real? Go to my blog, journalofanadhdkid.weebly.com/! Or check out my Facebook page, Journal of an ADHD Kid. Can't wait to hear from you online!

ACKNOWLEDGMENTS

A BIG THANK YOU to all my friends and family who helped me get this book done. A special thanks to those of you who read it to make sure it sounded okay, helped us edit our mistakes, make it better, and cheered us on. (You know who you are!) This is a very personal project, but it takes a lot of people to take it from inside my head and turn it into a book. Thank YOU!

AFTERWORD
BY HEATHER GOOCHEY, MS, LPCC

As the Director of a large mental health division that specializes in providing in-home mental health services to children and families, I have had the privilege of guiding the services of over eight hundred kids. Working with children and families who are learning to understand, accept, and live with ADHD has led me to realize that there is no such thing as "normal." Many of my clients experience the same struggles, joys, and confusion that Toby describes in his book.

Toby is a hero to many kids who feel that because of these four letters, A-D-H-D, they are not normal. He helps to show kids that despite these four letters, life is full of fun, family, and friends. Learning to live with the symptoms of ADHD is a lifelong journey that does not have to get in the way of anything! Any kid dealing with ADHD can find something in common with Toby, and parents can gain a great insight into their child's mind.

ABOUT THE AUTHORS

Stumpf family photo (Dawn, second from left; Toby, second from right)
Photo credit: Amy Shadduck Miller

Tobias (Toby) Stumpf lives in central Minnesota with his family...his dad, Jim, his sister, Talia, his mom, Dawn, and Baloo, his dog, Teresa the tortoise, and Philis and Pepper the chickens. He enjoys any sport with a board (snowboarding, skateboarding, and surfing) as well as basketball and golfing. Toby plays the drums and guitar. His favorite subject in school is science. He dreams of someday finding cures for things like cancer and ADHD!

Dawn Schaefer Stumpf is Tobias's mom. She is a graduate of St. Olaf College and St. Cloud State University. Dawn is an elementary educator. She is proud that Tobias was willing to talk about his ADHD through paper and pen. Dawn is honored to have shared the pen with him and blessed to call him her son!